A Career Day with an Engineer

Penelope Santos

I0808500

Rosen REAL READERS

Rosen Classroom™
New York

Engineers use math and science. They use these tools to solve problems. They build things that we need. They help make the world better.

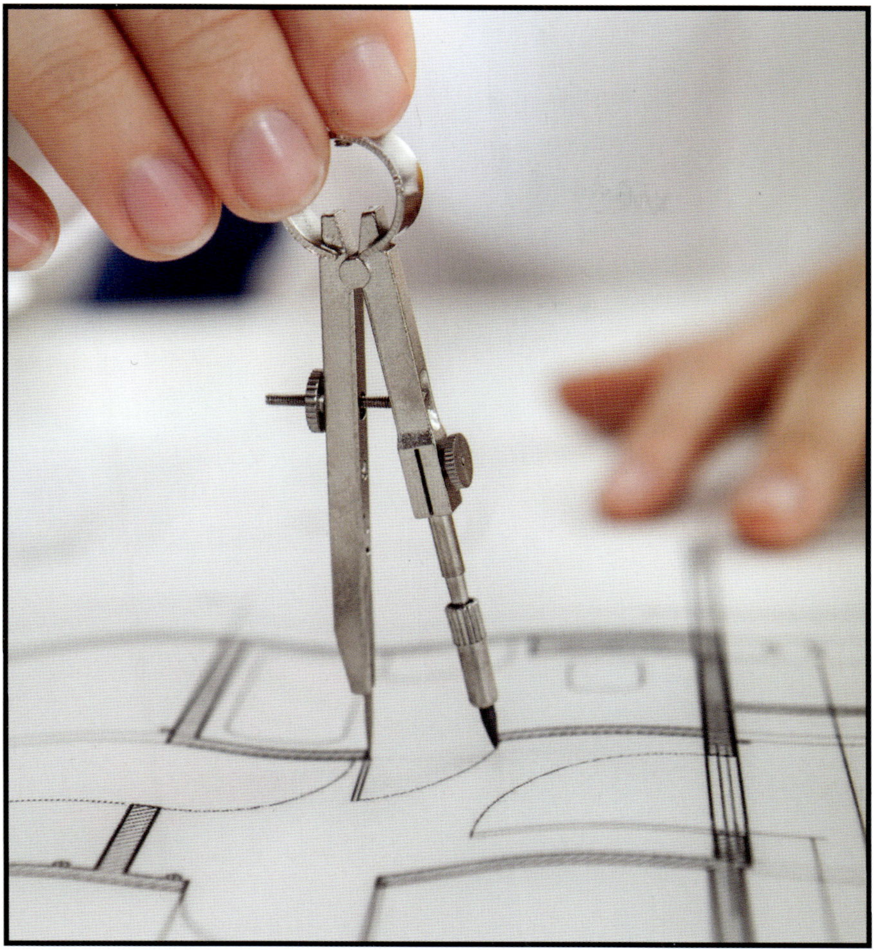

Engineers first design what they want to build. They make a model or a drawing. This engineer is drawing a house. He measures the angle of the door.

Aerospace engineers design things that fly. They design and build planes. They make planes safer and faster.

They also design and build spaceships. They create tools for astronauts to use, too. Spaceships take them to outer space.

Electrical engineers build machines that use energy. They use energy created by nature. The wind and the sun create natural energy.

They also design electronics in cars. Engineers design different switches. The switches turn things on and off.

Environmental engineers help improve our world. They think of ways to make it clean and safe. They think of ways to help clean up pollution.

Sometimes oil is spilled into a body of water. Engineers come up with ways to clean it. This river is being cleaned with their help.

Biomedical engineers use medicine and biology. They come up with new tools to make us healthy. They come up with ways to help sick people get better.

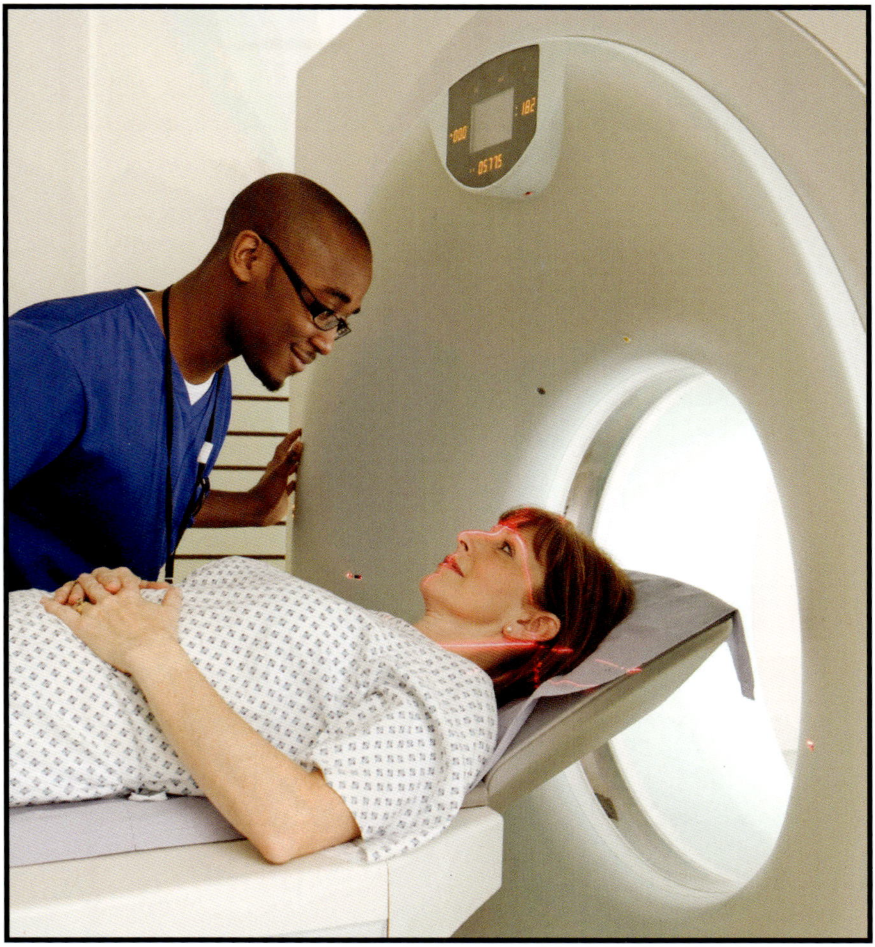

They design and build tools
like this special machine.
The machine helps the doctor
understand why a person is sick.

Words to Know

astronaut

drawing

math

plane

spaceship

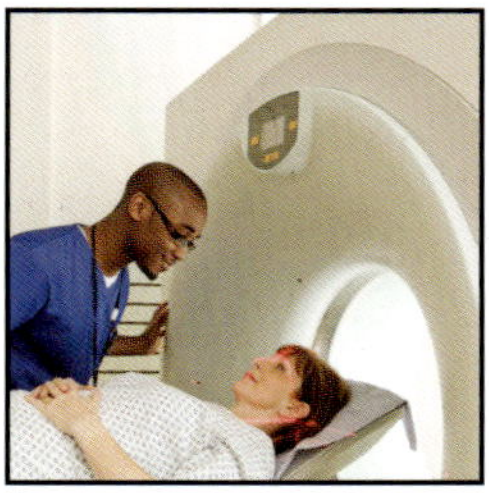

machine